Book of
Shadows

Book of Shadows

A journal to make magical discoveries

Silver Raven

SIRIUS

For Ruth

SIRIUS

This edition published in 2023 by Sirius Publishing, a division of
Arcturus Publishing Limited,
26/27 Bickels Yard, 151–153 Bermondsey Street,
London SE1 3HA

Designer: Sally Bond
Images: Shutterstock

ISBN: 978-1-3988-2067-8
AD010254UK

Printed in China

INTRODUCTION

What sort of magic do you practise? The sort I do is based on using the things I find around me. So perhaps a circular fallen leaf might put me in mind of a coin and be incorporated into a spell or ritual for money. Likewise, a piece of red fabric might be used in a charm for love.

When you work magic like this, the great thing is how personal it is. Our associations are formed by our thoughts, beliefs, culture, and upbringing. While fire might mean a joyous community event to one person, it could represent devastating forest fires, or an accidental fire that destroyed all their possessions, to another. So, the symbols we use are important in that they are personal to us. That is why I don't get too hung up on traditional correspondences for spells. Some traditions use them to great effect and that's wonderful, but I have my own system. The problem with it though is that it is like the cook who measures by sight and hand rather than following a recipe. This can make it hard to remember what you did to create that dish that everyone thought was spectacular. It may be that you think the moment of that dish being consumed is a sacred, once-in-a-lifetime one that shouldn't be repeated anyway, but I know I

miss my grandmother's potato-filled flatbreads and, now that she has passed, I am saddened that I will never taste them again.

A witch's book of shadows is like a recipe book that they might leave to a family member, although some are proponents of the tradition of burning a witch's book of shadows when she passes through the veil. You may use this journal to create your own book of shadows, which is personal to you. It will make it easier to check which spell or ritual worked for you and which didn't. In the first section you will find some information that is useful for magical work. For example, you will discover which are the best moon phases for different types of spells.

The rest of the journal is a series of blank and lined pages for you to fill with your own spells and magical findings. Use it to record significant dreams or sketch out sigils and symbols that you have been gifted through magical sight. Note down wondrous "coincidences" and stick in photos from enchanting places you have visited. Really make it your own!

Blessed be,
Silver Raven

Moon Phases

New Moon

This is the time to start new projects and do spells to attract new things into your life, be that a new job, relationship, or home.

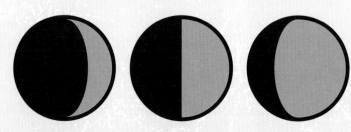

Waxing

This is the phase of expansion and is a fortunate time for growing businesses, becoming pregnant, and extending your home.

Full Moon

This is the witch's moon, when all things are possible. The light of this moon is sacred and it is good to leave spell ingredients overnight where the moonlight may fall upon them.

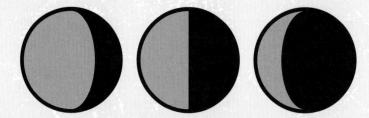

Waning Moon

This is the moon in which you bind, dispel, and end things with your magic. It is good for protection spells and for removing negative influences.

Witch's Toolkit

There are a number of items that it is always handy to have to hand when doing spell-work.

Candles

You can have a vast array of candles in lots of different hues that match the purpose of your spell, for example, red or pink for love, green for money and prosperity, and blue for health and healing. However, I tend to just keep a stack of white tealights as these are suitable for all spells.

Salt

Salt is one of the best purifiers around. You can use fancy pink and black salts, but even your everyday cooking salt is fine for casting a ring of purification around your space when doing spell-work or to use in protection and binding spells.

Wand

Many witches use a wand to direct energy. This might be an elaborate crystal-topped one, but a simple carved wooden wand from a suitable tree is one of

the most powerful tools you can have. Carve it yourself and pick a tree that you connect with, taking a naturally fallen branch to carve from.

Incense

Smell can transport you to another time and space. Use appropriate incense and essential oils to subtly welcome in the correct energies. For example, rose is suitable for romantic love, basil for prosperity, bergamot for success, and myrrh to communicate with the ancestors.

Water

A simple dish of water is good to keep on your altar as then all the elements are represented: candles for fire, salt for earth, your wand for spirit, and incense for air. This element can also be represented by running water if you live near to a stream or river that you can incorporate into your spell-work.

SCENT CORRESPONDENCES

You can find scents available in herb bundles, candles, essential oils, incenses, or salts. Speak to an aromatherapist about creating your own blend if you wish to combine more than one correspondence into a ritual or spell. Here are some common ones:

BASIL

to enhance wealth

BERGAMOT

to stimulate energy

JASMINE

to cure insomnia, remember happy memories

ORANGE

also good for physical energy and cheerfulness

EUCALYPTUS

releases negative energy from fights

LAVENDER

aids good sleep and encourages good-naturedness

CLARY SAGE

destresses and helps with acceptance

YLANG YLANG

promotes romantic love and enhances sexuality

RULES OF ATTRACTION

When working magic, you are essentially attracting outcomes to yourself—even a binding or banishing spell is attracting power to you. In order to retain that power, you need to ensure that your energy is clear. These five principles will begin that work for you.

1 GRATITUDE
Be thankful at all times for what you already have and then you can ask for further blessings. You can even use some of the pages at the back of this journal to write down all the things you're grateful for on any given day. This is especially handy on those days when you are feeling down and disconnected from grace.

2 KINDNESS
Show this to yourself and others. Don't push too hard when looking for outcomes—you don't have to conjure up the perfect life immediately. You can find 'perfect for you' bit by bit.

3 PERMISSION
Always ask any material/energy/spirit you work with to help you and listen carefully with your own energy to see if permission has been given for you to proceed.

4 FREE WILL
Don't try and bend anyone else to your will. Respect that the outcome you want to have happen may not be what someone else wants and may not even be in your best interests. Always leave room for divine energy to intervene in a good way for you.

5 WONDER
If you feel your sense of wonder slipping away, go look at whatever first caused you to pick up a book like this. What first sparked your interest in magic? You're not able to do magical things if you no longer believe in magic so keep yourself enchanted.

YOUR ENERGETIC MAKE-UP

Let's start to find out how your energy works. Answer the questions below as honestly as possible.

WOULD YOU DESCRIBE YOURSELF AS AN EXTROVERT OR AN INTROVERT?

_____

HOW TIRED DO YOU GET AFTER YOU'VE BEEN IN THE COMPANY OF PEOPLE?

_____

DO YOU OFTEN "FORGET" OR MISS THE MEDITATIONS AND MAGICAL PRACTICES THAT YOU WANT TO DO?

_____

_____

HOW PHYSICALLY ACTIVE ARE YOU?

_____

_____

_____

WHEN YOU BEGIN SPELL-WORK, WHAT DO YOU DO FIRST? HAVE A BATH? PLAY A PARTICULAR PIECE OF MUSIC? PERHAPS LIGHT A CANDLE OR BURN INCENSE? WHICH SENSE DO YOU EVOKE FIRST TO GET YOU IN THE RIGHT FRAME OF MIND?

_____

_____

_____

_____

_____

_____

_____

_____

_____

_____

_____

Think deeply about how you answered these questions and consciously observe what happens if you do the opposite for a while. The more you understand your energetic make-up, the more powerful your spells will be. For example, if you are naturally an introvert who finds the company of others tiring and who prefers light rather than strenuous exercise, a month in which you are expected to socialise and be outdoors a lot will not be the best time for you to do demanding rituals. However, a solo vacation during which you have time to think may be ideal for you to have the energetic space to do some effective spell-work. If you keep forgetting your magical practices, it can be a sign that you are out of alignment with your energetic body. Use your senses to bring yourself back into focus.

BUILDING A PICTURE OF MAGICAL YOU

In observing your energetic reactions, you will start to build up a picture of how you like to be in the world. If your personality and energetic make-up is that of a physically active extrovert, then you need to develop practices that match this. You may work well within a group or coven that do quite physical rituals once a month. Get online and find your people. If you are a more relaxed introvert, perhaps you need to do more meditative practices such as yoga and your magic might be better off being solitary and away from other people.

Finally, the most important question of all— how do you get into the right frame of mind before doing magical work.? The answer to this question will let you know which sense you like to employ to get into a magical state. For example, I myself am attuned to my sense of smell and so I only need to light some incense to cast a magical circle and begin spell-work.

RITUAL CLEANSING

Ritual cleansing is very important before embarking upon a magical practice. Most cultures have some form of bathing ritual—pick the one that feels most authentic to you and your traditions. For example, the Japanese have a bath ritual called *ofaru*, often done collectively at a public bathhouse called an *onsen*. Historically, the Romans also elevated bathing to a ritual art, building beautiful aqueducts near healing springs to enable bathers to take the waters.

Santeria, the African-Caribbean tradition that developed from the Yoruba West African religion, also relies heavily on a ritual bathing practice. Overleaf are a couple of baths that Santero Rivera, a priest within the tradition, gave me to help with clearing personal energy and appealing to the ancestors for help and guidance. You can use them yourself or adjust them to reflect the items you have available or the tradition you feel most comfortable working within. Your intent is the most important aspect.

The Queen's Bath

This is a bath primarily for those who identify as women, particularly those suffering from a lack of self-esteem or those regularly attracting unhappy circumstances such as bad relationships or difficult living situations.

Ingredients:

A cup of goat's milk

White or yellow gold flowers (no roses)

Florida water (you can get this online or in any store selling Caribbean or Latin American products—use the amount that feels right to you)

Honey

2 coconuts

Run a hot bath. Pour all the ingredients, except the honey and the water from one of the coconuts, into the bath. Do this with intent, knowing that you are asking your ancestors to bless the water that you are about to get into. Then crack the second coconut (I keep a hammer for cracking open coconuts—it is more potent than just buying coconut water as its energy is contained in the nut) and standing on a towel, pour the water over your head. Take the honey and rub it all over your body, concentrating on the belly and navel. Then get into the bath and soak, imagining that all psychic "dirt" is coming away in the water and all the good energy of the honey, flowers and perfumed water is entering your body. You can shower as normal afterwards. Thank your ancestors before you go to sleep that night.

Luck bath

This is suitable for everyone and it removes bad luck as well as strengthening your power. Have this bath early on a day that you don't mind having flowers and leaves dried upon you since you do not wash or brush off any remnants of this particular bath until the next day.

Ingredients:

Bunch of finely chopped basil
Bunch of finely chopped parsley
Petals from a bunch of flowers (avoid roses)
Florida water
Small bottle of whiskey
Pinch of tobacco

Mix the ingredients in a bowl and leave overnight covered with a white muslin cloth. In the morning, run a hot bath and sitting in that bath, ritually pour the bowl of bath ingredients over your head. It will feel cold, but you should feel fine about it since you are sat in a hot bath.

Do not submerge your head and resist the urge to wipe away any leaves left stuck to you. Sit close-eyed in the bath for a while thinking about what you would like to manifest in your life and the ways in which you seek protection from the spirits and your ancestors. If your belief system does not allow for spirits, deities, or ancestor guides, you can express gratitude to the secular universal energy that comprises us and all things. You should leave the flowers and leaves to dry on you naturally, only washing them off the next morning.

(Practical tip: get yourself a strainer for the bath drain to avoid leaves and flower petals blocking your pipes. Despite the sacred and ritual nature of these baths, you can put any waste leaves and petals in your compost or usual food disposal.)

NB: Roses are avoided because they have a special energy that, while used in some workings, are not compatible with the baths given here.

SETTING UP AN ALTAR

Your home is where you will create your magic and it needs to be able to support energy work. This means that you should have a clear, calm space in which to do spells. It goes without saying that clutter is not helpful when it comes to energy work; this is not because it isn't pretty to look at, but because of the guilt you feel when you look at something you have yet to deal with. Clutter is essentially decisions you aren't making so the first thing you have to do is trust yourself to make decisions regarding your stuff. This will support your trust in your own abilities to create the life you want or connect with the divinities you wish to contact.

Once you are rid of your clutter, you should also do a top to bottom clean of your home—or, at the very least, the room in which you intend to set up your altar. Try and use ecologically sound cleaning materials as you want to ensure that you are keeping the planet as clean and healthy as you want your home to be. A lot of old cleaning solutions are natural and only require effort.

You may then look around at your tidy and clean room and think that this is it. It is not. Everything is energetically charged as well. Cleaning and tidying begin to shift up the energetic dust, but it doesn't clean it up so you can have a perfectly clean and tidy space that

is energetically filthy because it is the scene of trauma or still holds repressed rage and other negative emotions.

There are several ways you can clear a space energetically. For example, you can:

★ smoke-cleanse a room by passing appropriate burning herbs or spices through it—sage is traditionally used for this purpose in Native American cultures, but you can also use rosemary, basil or cloves, depending on your own traditions

★ scatter sea salt over the carpet, ensuring you go into corners, leaving it for an hour or two, and then vacuuming it up

★ place a bowl of filtered water in each corner of the room, blow into each bowl while holding the intent to energetically clear the room into the water, leave for an hour, and then pour away the water into your lawn or a drain or running water

★ you can also clear a room with sound using either chanting, drumming, or even a handclap in each corner of the room as long as you visualise the sound-waves cleaning out the room's energy.

ALTAR SPACE

Begin by walking through your home looking for a space that would be perfect for your altar. Don't just look for practical things such as space on a shelf or mantel or the room that is the least used. Look also for how the space *feels*. As you develop your magical skills, you should be able to feel the energy of a part of the room and know whether this is an appropriate place for your altar. My altar is very low down and counterintuitive to where you would expect an altar to be. My father was surprised by it as, within his tradition, you never put anything sacred near the feet. Holy books and devotional prayer beads are all kept above the waist level

and ideally above the head. This is because the head is where divine energy first enters your body. However, in my tradition, every part of the body is sacred and equally connected to the divine. Therefore, I am perfectly fine kneeling at an altar that is virtually on the floor.

Once you have found the space you will use, you must clean it thoroughly. If it is a shelf, don't just wipe the shelf, check what is below it and behind it and ensure that there are no hidden cobwebs or dust there either. Then, using one of the methods on page 20, energetically clean the space as well.

FOCUS

To begin setting up your altar, you must first select the focus. This is an object that sits at the heart of your altar. Think about which element attracts you the most. You may find that the element connected with your astrological sun sign is the strongest for you.

FIRE
Aries, Leo,
Sagittarius

WATER
Cancer, Scorpio,
Pisces

EARTH
Taurus, Virgo,
Capricorn

AIR
Gemini, Libra,
Aquarius

For a focus that is linked to the element of fire, place a fireproof cauldron or bowl in the center of your altar. For water, a bowl of water. For earth, a bowl of earth or a plant. For air, you can choose a feather or the same as for fire since air feeds fire.

Once you have placed your chosen item at the center of your altar, take a deep breath in and out through your nose and then settle down in meditation in front of your altar. During your meditation, state your intent to use this altar to channel your energy and aid your magical work. Thank divine energy for enabling you to do the work.

Working with Candles

Candles should be chosen carefully with regard to type, and color, depending on the purpose of the spell. It is often better to use your intuition when choosing the type of candle, although for ease of reference, below is a list of the main types. There are other types available, but these are the most suitable for magical working.

Table

The most readily available candle, they are ideal for spell-working. They usually burn for six to eight hours and need to be properly seated in suitable candlesticks. All colors can be used (see pages 30-31 for correspondences), and they should be of the best quality possible.

Pillar

This is a free-standing candle. It is usually in the form of a simple pillar, although it can sometimes be made in other shapes which can be used as part of the spell, for example heart shapes for love spells. This type of candle is best burned on a flat holder since it usually takes some time to burn out.

Taper

These candles are tall and thin and need a particularly stable candle-holder. They are either made in a mould, or by the traditional method of dipping a length of wick into hot molten white or coloured wax. For magical purposes they should be colored all the way through. They can often be used when a quick result is required. Because they are quite fragile, you need to be careful not to break them when anointing them.

Tea lights

These small candles are excellent for use when a candle must be left to burn out, but are less easy to anoint with essential oils. Poured in small metal pots like small votives, they are normally used in oil burners or specially-made tea-light holders. Depending on their size, they burn for approximately four hours.

Votive

This type of candle is specially designed as an offering, to carry prayers to whichever deity you honour. As the wax melts, the holder, which is made of glass, can become hot so some care must be taken when using them. They are designed to be long-burning, usually between one and seven days.

Choosing your candles

There are several things you need to remember when choosing a candle:

1 Choose your candle type as opposite.

2 Candles used for magic should always be virgin (unused) at the start of the working, unless you have deliberately cleared them of past influences. Using candles that have been previously lit can have a detrimental effect on your spell. They may have picked up influences from previous use.

3 Charge your candle before using it. This can be done by anointing it with oils associated with the magic you intend on performing, or by simply touching it and filling it with your own energy.

4 The oils used in the anointing of your candle should, where possible, always be natural fragrances. While charging the candle, smooth from top to bottom when drawing energy toward you, bottom to top when sending energy outwards. Particularly when anointing candles for altar use, anoint from the middle to the top and from the middle to the bottom to signify the union of spiritual and physical realms.

5 If you enjoy craftwork, it is a very good idea to make your own candles for magical use. It is a whole art in itself—you infuse your candles with your own energy and thus increase the magical potency of the candle many times over. It is relatively easy to make your own candles: simply heat the wax until it is liquid and pour into a mould which is threaded with a wick. The wax should now be left to cool, after which the mould can be removed. Oils and colors can be added for extra potency.

Dressing and charging candles

Dressing (anointing) and charging candles are perhaps candle magic in its simplest form. Dressing a candle performs two functions. By anointing it with oil you ensure that it burns safely and you also have the opportunity to infuse it with the required vibration for your working. Charging a candle ensures you fix the intent of your magical working and also dedicates the candle to the appropriate purpose.

DRESSING CANDLES

Any oil can be used for dressing a candle but initially it is best to use either your favourite essential oil, such as frankincense, or perhaps an oil infused with a suitable herb appropriate to the task in hand.

There are various ways to dress a candle but what is important is the direction in which you anoint it. If you remember that working from the top down draws in power from spiritual sources, and working from the bottom up draws in energy from the earth, it is very easy to work correctly for your purpose. Never rub the candle with a back and forth movement, as you will end up with a confusion of energies—and a sputtering candle.

YOU WILL NEED

Candle

Oil

METHOD

★ Sit quietly and, holding the candle, think carefully about your intent. If you have learned to meditate, then enter a meditative state and allow the energies to build up within you.
★ To bring something to you, rub oil on the candle in a downward motion from the top to the bottom.
★ To send something away from you, you rub the oil from the bottom to the top.
★ Continue with either movement until you have a sense that you have done enough. If you have any oil left on your hands either rub your hands together until the oil is absorbed or dab the remaining oil from your fingers onto the center of your forehead, which is the Third Eye and the seat of vision. Then say the following or something similar:

I cleanse and consecrate this candle (in the name of your chosen deity, if you choose to use one).

May it burn with strength in the service of the Greater Good.

★ Your candle is now ready for use.

CHARGING CANDLES

This is a quick, uncomplicated method of more fully charging a candle. This method can be used without having to set up your altar completely. It can equally be used to charge your altar candles.

YOU WILL NEED

A candle or candles of the appropriate color (if preferred, mark them with appropriate symbols)

A candle holder

Matches rather than a lighter

METHOD

★ Hold the candle in your 'power hand' (the hand you consider you give out energy with).

★ Open the other hand and turn that palm towards the sky.

★ Breathe deeply and visualize your goal.

★ Now perceive whatever you think of as universal energy flowing through the palm that is turned skyward, filling your body.

★ Visualise that universal energy mixing within you with the energy of your intention.

★ Now allow that mixed energy to flow into the candle.

★ Be conscious of the energy as it builds up.

★ Feel the energy streaming into the candle.

★ Fill it from bottom to top as though the candle were an empty vessel.

★ If you are comfortable with doing so, speak your intention out loud.

★ As you place the candle in its holder, stabilize the thought within the candle so that it will be converted into pure clear intent.

★ Strike a match above the candle.

★ Draw down the flame toward the candle, lighting the wick.

★ Extinguish the match flame, but do not blow it out in case you blow out the candle.

★ Stay with the candle for a few moments visualizing your intention, feeling its energy moving into the universe.

★ Leave the area and let the candle burn right down as it does its work.

Candle color and the symbols inscribed on them create additional power. As you become more proficient, you will find yourself using certain colors and symbols more often. Try not to be too rigid, and always be open to widening your focus.

Candle Correspondences

Many different colors are used in candle magic and below are listed the most common ones, along with their key associations and purposes. White can be used as a substitute if your chosen color is not available, since it contains all the colors.

White

★ The Goddess
★ Protection
★ Purity
★ Peace

Black

★ Binding
★ Mediumship
★ Protection
★ Repels negativity

Brown

★ Material luck
★ To influence friendships
★ Healing earth energies

Orange

★ General success
★ Property deals
★ Legal matters
★ Justice
★ Selling

Purple

★ Third eye
★ Psychic ability
★ Hidden knowledge
★ To influence people in high places
★ Spiritual power

Pink

★ Affection
★ Romance
★ Caring
★ Nurturing
★ Care for the planet

BLUE

★ The Element of Water
★ Wisdom
★ Calm
★ Good fortune
★ Opening communication
★ Spiritual inspiration

GREEN

★ The Element of Earth
★ Physical healing
★ Monetary success
★ Mother Earth
★ Tree and plant magic
★ Growth
★ Personal goals

RED

★ The Element of Fire
★ Passion
★ Strength
★ Fast action
★ Career goals
★ Lust
★ Driving force
★ Survival

GOLD

★ The Sun God
★ Promote winning
★ Male power
★ Happiness

SILVER

★ The Moon Goddess
★ Astral energy
★ Female energy
★ Telepathy
★ Clairvoyance
★ Intuition
★ Dreams

YELLOW

★ The Element of Air
★ Intelligence
★ The Sun
★ Memory
★ Imagination supported by logic
★ Accelerating learning
★ Clearing mental blocks

COPPER

★ Professional growth
★ Business productivity
★ Career success
★ Passion
★ Money goals

SIGNS FROM CANDLE-BURNING

Not every magical practitioner takes heed of the manner in which spell-casting or ritual candles burn; there is often a great deal to be learnt from understanding a little bit more about how to interpret the way a candle burns.

It is worth remembering that some candles are simply poorly made and will burn badly no matter what you do with them. If the wick is the wrong size, for instance, the candle may be of no use for magical work. It is nice to make one's own candles, although there is quite an art to it and the novice may end up feeling rather frustrated, if the candle is not quite right.

External factors can also play a huge part in how candles burn. The way the candle is placed in the holder, the temperature in the surrounding area, an open window causing a draught, and other such things can all make a difference. Equally, the candle can be affected by your own mood and, until you have learned how to meditate using a candle flame, you need not worry too much to begin with. All that having been said, here are some of the things to watch for when burning candles.

The candle gives a clean, even burn This might be called a successful burn and suggests the spell will most likely achieve the right result. If a glass-encased candle burns and leaves no marks on the glass that is best. If a free-standing candle leaves little or no residue, this is by far the best result.

The flame flares, dips, gutters, repeatedly Check first for draughts and then decide intuitively whether there is a pattern to the flaring and guttering. If you are performing the spell with someone in mind, you may feel the recipient of your spell is trying to block your efforts. Sit quietly for a while until you feel you have grasped the significance of the pattern, which may be because the spell itself is not right for the time. In this case simply be prepared to try again another time.

A free-standing candle runs and melts a lot while burning This gives you an opportunity to observe the flow of wax for signs. Quickly melting wax shows there is a good deal of positivity available. If one side burns quicker than the other, a balance can sometimes be achieved by turning the candle round and it is useful to note how many times you do this, since this can indicate the number of adjustments the person may have to make to ensure success. Other people prefer to let nature take its course and to watch the wax run for signs, without interfering in its movements.

A free-standing candle burns down to a puddle of wax or sets in runs down the side of the candle When this happens, most workers will examine the shape of the wax for a sign. For instance, a heart-shaped wax puddle is a good sign if you are burning a red candle for a love spell. You may see something of importance there, for the shape of the run may suggest an outcome regarding the matter at hand. Wax puddles come in all kinds of shapes; most candle-workers look for symbols in the wax, or sometimes use numerology or other divination techniques, similar to teacup reading, to discover meaning.

A glass-encased candle burns clean to begin with but "dirty" with a great deal of smoke later This indicates that things will go well to begin with, but there are other conditions that have not yet revealed themselves and will need to be resolved. Someone may be working against the required outcome, so care over the correct timing and correspondences of further spells is crucial.

A free-standing candle lets out a lot of smoke but burns clean at the end Difficult conditions need to be dealt with first of all but eventually conditions improve. Look for what you can practically do to aid the successful completion of the spell.

There is a dirty, black burn (especially one that deposits soot on a glass-encased candle) This means things are not going to go well—the spell may not work, the blessing may fail, the person is in deeper stress or trouble than you first thought. There is a great deal of negativity around. Sometimes it is good to change the focus of the candle and ask that it be used to burn off the negativity, which will enable you to get a handle on the situation.

The candle goes out before completely burning This can mean that the spell you are using is not the most appropriate one and you need to use stronger means than you first employed. It can also mean that someone is actively working against you. In this case it is wise to go back to the beginning and start your whole spell over again.

The candle tips over and flames up into a potential fire hazard Provided that you know you have placed the candles properly, this indicates there is danger about for you or the person you are casting for. You should clear your sacred space and cleanse it by whatever means you prefer. It is probably wise to wait a while before retrying the spell and remember to take a ritual bath (see pages 15–19) before you do.

The candle burns too quickly Generally a fast burn is good, but an overly fast burn means that, although the work will go well, its effect will not last long. Again, you might wait before retrying the spell, though sometimes a fast result is required. You should use your own judgement.

DISPOSAL OF CANDLE WAX

In European-American traditions, many people bury candle wax and other remains after a spell is cast. Burial toward the appropriate quarter of the compass is considered a thoughtful way to go about this. Some Pagans dispose of ritual or spell remains in a bonfire or fireplace.

DATE: _____

SPELL/RITUAL FOR: _____

TOOLS USED: _____

_____

_____

WHAT I DID: _____

_____

_____

_____

_____

_____

_____

_____

_____

_____

_____

_____

_____

_____

WHAT WAS THE OUTCOME?

DATE: _____

SPELL/RITUAL FOR: _____

TOOLS USED: _____

_____

_____

WHAT I DID: _____

_____

_____

_____

_____

_____

_____

_____

_____

_____

_____

_____

_____

WHAT WAS THE OUTCOME?

_____

_____

_____

_____

_____

_____

_____

_____

_____

_____

_____

_____

_____

_____

_____

_____

DATE: _____

SPELL/RITUAL FOR: _____

TOOLS USED: _____

_____

_____

WHAT I DID: _____

_____

_____

_____

_____

_____

_____

_____

_____

_____

_____

_____

_____

_____

_____

WHAT WAS THE OUTCOME?

_____

_____

_____

_____

_____

_____

_____

_____

_____

_____

_____

_____

_____

_____

_____

_____

_____

_____

_____

_____

DATE: _____

SPELL/RITUAL FOR: _____

TOOLS USED: _____

_____

_____

WHAT I DID: _____

_____

_____

_____

_____

_____

_____

_____

_____

_____

_____

_____

_____

_____

WHAT WAS THE OUTCOME?

_____

_____

_____

_____

_____

_____

_____

_____

_____

_____

_____

_____

_____

_____

_____

_____

DATE: _____

SPELL/RITUAL FOR: _____

TOOLS USED: _____

_____

_____

WHAT I DID: _____

_____

_____

_____

_____

_____

_____

_____

_____

_____

_____

_____

_____

_____

_____

WHAT WAS THE OUTCOME?

_____

_____

_____

_____

_____

_____

_____

_____

_____

_____

_____

_____

_____

_____

_____

_____

_____

DATE: _____

SPELL/RITUAL FOR: _____

TOOLS USED: _____

_____

_____

WHAT I DID: _____

_____

_____

_____

_____

_____

_____

_____

_____

_____

_____

_____

_____

_____

_____

WHAT WAS THE OUTCOME?

_____

_____

_____

_____

_____

_____

_____

_____

_____

_____

_____

_____

_____

_____

_____

_____

_____

_____

DATE: _____

SPELL/RITUAL FOR: _____

TOOLS USED: _____

_____

_____

WHAT I DID: _____

_____

_____

_____

_____

_____

_____

_____

_____

_____

_____

_____

_____

WHAT WAS THE OUTCOME?

_____

_____

_____

_____

_____

_____

_____

_____

_____

_____

_____

_____

_____

_____

_____

_____

DATE: _____

SPELL/RITUAL FOR: _____

TOOLS USED: _____

_____

_____

WHAT I DID: _____

_____

_____

_____

_____

_____

_____

_____

_____

_____

_____

_____

_____

WHAT WAS THE OUTCOME?

_____
_____
_____
_____
_____
_____
_____
_____
_____
_____
_____
_____
_____
_____
_____
_____
_____
_____

DATE: _____

SPELL/RITUAL FOR: _____

TOOLS USED: _____

_____

_____

WHAT I DID: _____

_____

_____

_____

_____

_____

_____

_____

_____

_____

_____

_____

WHAT WAS THE OUTCOME?

DATE: _____

SPELL/RITUAL FOR: _____

TOOLS USED: _____

_____

_____

WHAT I DID: _____

_____

_____

_____

_____

_____

_____

_____

_____

_____

_____

What was the outcome?

_____

_____

_____

_____

_____

_____

_____

_____

_____

_____

_____

_____

_____

_____

_____

DATE: _____

SPELL/RITUAL FOR: _____

TOOLS USED: _____

_____

_____

WHAT I DID: _____

_____

_____

_____

_____

_____

_____

_____

_____

_____

_____

_____

_____

_____

WHAT WAS THE OUTCOME?

_____

_____

_____

_____

_____

_____

_____

_____

_____

_____

_____

_____

_____

_____

_____

_____

_____

_____

DATE: _____

SPELL/RITUAL FOR: _____

TOOLS USED: _____

_____

_____

WHAT I DID: _____

_____

_____

_____

_____

_____

_____

_____

_____

_____

_____

WHAT WAS THE OUTCOME?

DATE: _____

SPELL/RITUAL FOR: _____

TOOLS USED: _____

_____

_____

WHAT I DID: _____

_____

_____

_____

_____

_____

_____

_____

_____

_____

_____

_____

_____

_____

WHAT WAS THE OUTCOME?

_____

_____

_____

_____

_____

_____

_____

_____

_____

_____

_____

_____

_____

_____

_____

_____

_____

DATE: _____

SPELL/RITUAL FOR: _____

TOOLS USED: _____

_____

WHAT I DID: _____

_____

_____

_____

_____

_____

_____

_____

_____

_____

_____

_____

_____

WHAT WAS THE OUTCOME?

_____

_____

_____

_____

_____

_____

_____

_____

_____

_____

_____

_____

_____

_____

_____

_____

_____

DATE: _____

SPELL/RITUAL FOR: _____

TOOLS USED: _____

_____

WHAT I DID: _____

_____

_____

_____

_____

_____

_____

_____

_____

_____

_____

WHAT WAS THE OUTCOME?

DATE: _____

SPELL/RITUAL FOR: _____

TOOLS USED: _____

_____

WHAT I DID: _____

_____

_____

_____

_____

_____

_____

_____

_____

_____

_____

_____

WHAT WAS THE OUTCOME?

_____

_____

_____

_____

_____

_____

_____

_____

_____

_____

_____

_____

_____

_____

_____

_____

_____

_____